55 Around the Grill: BBQ and Beyond Recipes for Home

By: Kelly Johnson

Table of Contents

Grilled Meats:

- Classic Grilled Steak with Garlic Butter
- BBQ Chicken Skewers with Tangy Marinade
- Honey Mustard Glazed Grilled Pork Chops
- Smoky Chipotle Grilled Shrimp
- Teriyaki Glazed Grilled Salmon
- Lemon Herb Grilled Chicken Thighs
- Tandoori-Style Grilled Lamb Chops
- Pineapple Sriracha Grilled Pork Tenderloin
- Coffee-Rubbed Grilled Ribeye
- Grilled Bratwurst with Beer-Braised Onions

Burger Creations:

- Ultimate Bacon BBQ Burger
- Portobello Mushroom Veggie Burger
- Southwest Chipotle Turkey Burgers
- Blue Cheese-Stuffed Grilled Buffalo Chicken Burger
- Hawaiian Teriyaki Pineapple Burger
- Greek Lamb Burgers with Tzatziki Sauce
- Tex-Mex BBQ Black Bean Burger
- Salmon Avocado Burger with Dill Mayo
- Pesto Caprese Chicken Burger
- BBQ Pulled Pork Sliders

Grilled Vegetables:

- Balsamic Glazed Grilled Vegetables
- Grilled Zucchini Ribbons with Parmesan
- Cajun Spiced Grilled Corn on the Cob
- Mediterranean Grilled Eggplant
- Honey Sriracha Grilled Brussels Sprouts
- Grilled Asparagus with Lemon Zest
- Mexican Street Corn (Elote)

- Herb-Marinated Grilled Portobello Mushrooms
- Grilled Sweet Potato Wedges
- Teriyaki Glazed Grilled Pineapple

Seafood Delights:

- Grilled Lobster Tails with Garlic Butter
- Tequila Lime Grilled Shrimp Tacos
- Citrus-Marinated Grilled Swordfish
- Grilled Scallop Skewers with Lemon-Herb Drizzle
- Cajun Grilled Catfish Fillets
- Chimichurri Grilled Octopus
- Thai Coconut Lemongrass Grilled Mussels
- Grilled Oysters with Garlic Parmesan Butter
- Grilled Clams with White Wine and Garlic
- Grilled Teriyaki Tuna Steaks

Side and Accompaniments:

- Grilled Caesar Salad with Homemade Croutons
- Smoked Mac and Cheese
- Grilled Stuffed Jalapeños with Cream Cheese
- Barbecue Baked Beans with Bacon
- Grilled Avocado with Salsa
- Garlic Butter Grilled Naan Bread
- Caprese Skewers with Balsamic Glaze
- Grilled Watermelon Salad with Feta
- BBQ Grilled Potato Packets
- Pimento Cheese-Stuffed Grilled Mushrooms

Sauces and Marinades:

- Homemade BBQ Sauce with a Kick
- Chimichurri Sauce for Grilled Meats
- Thai Peanut Sauce for Grilled Satay
- Honey-Soy Glaze for Grilled Chicken
- Bourbon Maple Glaze for Grilled Pork

Grilled Meats:

Classic Grilled Steak with Garlic Butter

Ingredients:

For the Steak:

- 2 ribeye or sirloin steaks (about 1 inch thick)
- Salt and black pepper to taste
- 2 tablespoons olive oil

For the Garlic Butter:

- 1/2 cup unsalted butter, softened
- 4 cloves garlic, minced
- 1 tablespoon fresh parsley, chopped
- Salt to taste

Instructions:

1. Preparing the Steak:

    Preheat the Grill:
    - Preheat your grill to medium-high heat.

    Season the Steaks:
    - Take the steaks out of the refrigerator and let them come to room temperature for about 30 minutes.
    - Pat the steaks dry with paper towels to remove excess moisture.
    - Season both sides of the steaks with salt and black pepper. Drizzle olive oil over the steaks and rub it in.

    Grilling the Steaks:
    - Place the steaks on the preheated grill. For medium-rare, grill for about 4-5 minutes per side, depending on the thickness of the steaks and your desired doneness.
    - Adjust the cooking time for your preferred level of doneness (medium, medium-well, well-done).

    Resting the Steaks:

- Once done, remove the steaks from the grill and let them rest for 5-10 minutes. This allows the juices to redistribute, ensuring a juicy and flavorful steak.

2. Making the Garlic Butter:

   Prepare Garlic Butter Mixture:
   - In a bowl, combine the softened butter, minced garlic, chopped parsley, and a pinch of salt. Mix well until all ingredients are thoroughly incorporated.

   Forming a Butter Log:
   - Place the garlic butter mixture on a piece of plastic wrap. Roll it into a log shape and refrigerate until firm.

3. Serving:

   Serving the Steak:
   - Slice the grilled steak against the grain into thin strips.

   Adding Garlic Butter:
   - Place a slice of the garlic butter log on top of the hot steak slices. The butter will melt and infuse the steak with rich flavor.

   Garnish and Serve:
   - Garnish with additional chopped parsley if desired.
   - Serve the classic grilled steak with garlic butter alongside your favorite grilled vegetables, potatoes, or a fresh salad.

Enjoy this classic grilled steak with garlic butter for a delicious and satisfying meal!

BBQ Chicken Skewers with Tangy Marinade

Ingredients:

For the Marinade:

- 1.5 lbs (about 700g) boneless, skinless chicken thighs, cut into bite-sized pieces
- 1/4 cup soy sauce
- 2 tablespoons tomato paste
- 2 tablespoons honey or maple syrup
- 2 tablespoons Dijon mustard
- 2 tablespoons apple cider vinegar
- 2 cloves garlic, minced
- 1 teaspoon smoked paprika
- 1 teaspoon ground cumin
- 1 teaspoon onion powder
- Salt and black pepper to taste

For Skewers:

- Wooden or metal skewers (if using wooden skewers, soak them in water for 30 minutes to prevent burning)

For Garnish (optional):

- Fresh parsley or cilantro, chopped

Instructions:

1. Prepare the Marinade:

   In a bowl, whisk together soy sauce, tomato paste, honey (or maple syrup), Dijon mustard, apple cider vinegar, minced garlic, smoked paprika, ground cumin, onion powder, salt, and black pepper.
   Taste the marinade and adjust the sweetness or saltiness according to your preference.

Place the chicken pieces in a ziplock bag or a shallow dish, and pour the marinade over them. Ensure the chicken is well-coated. Marinate for at least 2 hours, or preferably overnight in the refrigerator.

2. Skewering the Chicken:

Preheat your grill or grill pan to medium-high heat.
Thread the marinated chicken pieces onto the skewers.
If you're using wooden skewers, make sure to leave a bit of space between each piece for even cooking.

3. Grilling the Skewers:

Brush the grill grates with oil to prevent sticking.
Place the skewers on the preheated grill and cook for about 8-10 minutes, turning occasionally, until the chicken is fully cooked and has a nice char.
Baste the skewers with any remaining marinade during the last few minutes of cooking.

4. Garnish and Serve:

Once cooked, remove the skewers from the grill.
Garnish with chopped fresh parsley or cilantro, if desired.
Serve the BBQ chicken skewers with your favorite side dishes like rice, grilled vegetables, or a refreshing salad.

Enjoy these BBQ Chicken Skewers with a delicious and tangy marinade at your next barbecue or gathering!

Honey Mustard Glazed Grilled Pork Chops

Ingredients:

For the Pork Chops:

- 4 bone-in pork chops (about 1 inch thick)
- Salt and black pepper to taste
- 2 tablespoons olive oil

For the Honey Mustard Glaze:

- 1/4 cup Dijon mustard
- 2 tablespoons honey
- 2 tablespoons whole grain mustard
- 2 tablespoons soy sauce
- 2 cloves garlic, minced
- 1 teaspoon paprika
- 1/2 teaspoon dried thyme (optional)

Instructions:

1. Preparing the Pork Chops:

    Pat the pork chops dry with paper towels. Season both sides with salt and black pepper.
    Rub the pork chops with olive oil, ensuring they are well-coated.
    Allow the pork chops to come to room temperature while you prepare the glaze.

2. Making the Honey Mustard Glaze:

    In a bowl, whisk together Dijon mustard, honey, whole grain mustard, soy sauce, minced garlic, paprika, and dried thyme (if using). Mix until well combined.
    Taste the glaze and adjust the sweetness or saltiness according to your preference.

3. Grilling the Pork Chops:

Preheat your grill to medium-high heat.
Place the pork chops on the preheated grill. Cook for about 4-5 minutes per side for medium doneness, adjusting the time according to your preferred level of doneness.
During the last few minutes of grilling, brush the honey mustard glaze onto both sides of the pork chops, allowing it to caramelize.
Ensure the internal temperature of the pork chops reaches 145°F (63°C) for safe consumption.

4. Resting and Serving:

Remove the pork chops from the grill and let them rest for a few minutes.
Serve the Honey Mustard Glazed Grilled Pork Chops hot, drizzled with any remaining glaze.
Garnish with fresh herbs or a sprinkle of sesame seeds if desired.

Enjoy these flavorful and juicy Honey Mustard Glazed Grilled Pork Chops with your favorite sides, such as roasted vegetables, mashed potatoes, or a crisp salad!

Smoky Chipotle Grilled Shrimp

Ingredients:

For the Marinade:

- 1 pound large shrimp, peeled and deveined
- 3 tablespoons olive oil
- 2 tablespoons chipotle peppers in adobo sauce, minced
- 2 tablespoons fresh lime juice
- 2 cloves garlic, minced
- 1 teaspoon ground cumin
- 1 teaspoon smoked paprika
- 1 teaspoon dried oregano
- Salt and black pepper to taste
- Wooden or metal skewers (if using wooden skewers, soak them in water for 30 minutes)

For Garnish:

- Fresh cilantro, chopped
- Lime wedges

Instructions:

1. Marinating the Shrimp:

    In a bowl, combine olive oil, minced chipotle peppers, fresh lime juice, minced garlic, ground cumin, smoked paprika, dried oregano, salt, and black pepper. Mix well to form the marinade.
    Add the peeled and deveined shrimp to the marinade, ensuring they are well-coated. Cover and refrigerate for at least 30 minutes to allow the flavors to infuse.

2. Skewering and Grilling:

    Preheat your grill to medium-high heat.
    Thread the marinated shrimp onto the skewers, leaving a bit of space between each shrimp for even cooking.
    Brush the grill grates with oil to prevent sticking.

Place the shrimp skewers on the preheated grill and cook for approximately 2-3 minutes per side, or until the shrimp turn opaque and have a nice grill mark.

3. Garnish and Serve:

   Remove the shrimp skewers from the grill.
   Garnish with freshly chopped cilantro and serve with lime wedges on the side.
   Serve the Smoky Chipotle Grilled Shrimp as an appetizer or as part of a main course with your favorite side dishes.

Enjoy these smoky, spicy, and flavorful grilled shrimp at your next barbecue or gathering!

Teriyaki Glazed Grilled Salmon

Ingredients:

For the Teriyaki Glaze:

- 1/4 cup soy sauce
- 3 tablespoons mirin (Japanese sweet rice wine)
- 2 tablespoons sake (or dry white wine)
- 2 tablespoons brown sugar
- 1 tablespoon honey
- 1 tablespoon grated fresh ginger
- 2 cloves garlic, minced
- 1 teaspoon cornstarch (optional, for thickening)

For the Grilled Salmon:

- 4 salmon fillets (about 6 ounces each)
- Salt and black pepper to taste
- Sesame seeds and chopped green onions for garnish (optional)
- Lime wedges for serving

Instructions:

1. Prepare the Teriyaki Glaze:

    In a small saucepan, combine soy sauce, mirin, sake, brown sugar, honey, grated ginger, and minced garlic.
    Bring the mixture to a simmer over medium heat, stirring occasionally.
    If you prefer a thicker glaze, mix cornstarch with a tablespoon of water to create a slurry. Stir the slurry into the teriyaki sauce, and continue to simmer until it thickens. Remove from heat and let it cool.

2. Grilling the Salmon:

    Preheat your grill to medium-high heat.
    Season the salmon fillets with salt and black pepper.
    Place the salmon fillets on the preheated grill, skin side down. Grill for about 3-4 minutes per side, or until the salmon is cooked to your desired level of doneness.

Brush the teriyaki glaze onto the salmon during the last couple of minutes of grilling, allowing it to caramelize.

3. Garnish and Serve:

　　Transfer the grilled salmon to a serving platter.
　　Drizzle additional teriyaki glaze over the salmon fillets.
　　Garnish with sesame seeds and chopped green onions if desired.
　　Serve the Teriyaki Glazed Grilled Salmon hot, with lime wedges on the side.

Enjoy this flavorful and succulent teriyaki-glazed grilled salmon with the perfect balance of sweetness and umami!

Lemon Herb Grilled Chicken Thighs

Ingredients:

For the Marinade:

- 8 bone-in, skin-on chicken thighs
- 1/4 cup olive oil
- 1/4 cup fresh lemon juice
- Zest of 1 lemon
- 3 cloves garlic, minced
- 1 tablespoon fresh thyme, chopped
- 1 tablespoon fresh rosemary, chopped
- 1 teaspoon dried oregano
- Salt and black pepper to taste

For Garnish:

- Fresh parsley, chopped
- Lemon wedges for serving

Instructions:

1. Prepare the Marinade:

    In a bowl, whisk together olive oil, fresh lemon juice, lemon zest, minced garlic, chopped thyme, chopped rosemary, dried oregano, salt, and black pepper.
    Place the chicken thighs in a large ziplock bag or a shallow dish.
    Pour the marinade over the chicken thighs, ensuring they are well-coated. Seal the bag or cover the dish and refrigerate for at least 2 hours, or preferably overnight for more flavor.

2. Grilling the Chicken Thighs:

    Preheat your grill to medium-high heat.
    Remove the chicken thighs from the marinade and let them come to room temperature for about 15-20 minutes.

Grill the chicken thighs, skin side down, for approximately 6-8 minutes per side, or until the internal temperature reaches 165°F (74°C).
Baste the chicken thighs with any remaining marinade during the last few minutes of grilling.

3. Garnish and Serve:

　　Transfer the grilled chicken thighs to a serving platter.
　　Garnish with chopped fresh parsley.
　　Serve the Lemon Herb Grilled Chicken Thighs hot, accompanied by lemon wedges on the side.

Enjoy these flavorful and juicy grilled chicken thighs with the bright and aromatic combination of lemon and herbs!

Tandoori-Style Grilled Lamb Chops

Ingredients:

For the Marinade:

- 8 lamb chops
- 1 cup plain yogurt
- 2 tablespoons ginger-garlic paste
- 2 tablespoons Tandoori masala spice blend
- 1 tablespoon ground cumin
- 1 tablespoon ground coriander
- 1 teaspoon turmeric powder
- 1 teaspoon smoked paprika
- 1 teaspoon red chili powder (adjust to taste)
- Salt to taste
- 2 tablespoons lemon juice
- 2 tablespoons vegetable oil

For Garnish:

- Fresh cilantro, chopped
- Lemon wedges

Instructions:

1. Prepare the Marinade:

    In a bowl, combine yogurt, ginger-garlic paste, Tandoori masala spice blend, ground cumin, ground coriander, turmeric powder, smoked paprika, red chili powder, salt, lemon juice, and vegetable oil. Mix well to form a smooth marinade. Place the lamb chops in a large shallow dish or a ziplock bag.
    Pour the marinade over the lamb chops, ensuring they are well-coated. Massage the marinade into the meat.
    Cover the dish or seal the bag, and refrigerate for at least 2 hours, or preferably overnight for more intense flavors.

2. Grilling the Lamb Chops:

    Preheat your grill to medium-high heat.

Remove the lamb chops from the marinade and let them come to room temperature for about 15-20 minutes.

Grill the lamb chops for approximately 4-5 minutes per side, or until they reach your desired level of doneness.

Baste the lamb chops with any remaining marinade during the last few minutes of grilling.

3. Garnish and Serve:

Transfer the grilled lamb chops to a serving platter.

Garnish with chopped fresh cilantro.

Serve the Tandoori-Style Grilled Lamb Chops hot, accompanied by lemon wedges on the side.

Enjoy the authentic flavors of Tandoori-style grilled lamb chops with the perfect blend of spices!

Pineapple Sriracha Grilled Pork Tenderloin

Ingredients:

For the Marinade:

- 1 pork tenderloin (about 1 to 1.5 lbs)
- 1 cup pineapple juice
- 1/4 cup soy sauce
- 2 tablespoons Sriracha sauce (adjust to taste)
- 3 tablespoons honey
- 2 tablespoons olive oil
- 2 cloves garlic, minced
- 1 teaspoon ground ginger
- Salt and black pepper to taste

For Glazing (optional):

- Extra honey for glazing

For Garnish:

- Fresh cilantro, chopped
- Pineapple slices

Instructions:

1. Prepare the Marinade:

    In a bowl, whisk together pineapple juice, soy sauce, Sriracha sauce, honey, olive oil, minced garlic, ground ginger, salt, and black pepper.
    Place the pork tenderloin in a ziplock bag or a shallow dish.
    Pour the marinade over the pork, ensuring it's well-coated. Seal the bag or cover the dish, and refrigerate for at least 2 hours, or preferably overnight.

2. Grilling the Pork Tenderloin:

    Preheat your grill to medium-high heat.

Remove the pork tenderloin from the marinade and let it come to room temperature for about 15-20 minutes.

Grill the pork tenderloin for about 15-20 minutes, turning occasionally, or until the internal temperature reaches 145°F (63°C). Baste with the remaining marinade during grilling.

Optional: In the last few minutes of grilling, brush the pork with extra honey for a sweet glaze.

3. Resting and Garnishing:

Remove the grilled pork tenderloin from the grill and let it rest for about 5 minutes.

Slice the pork into medallions.

4. Garnish and Serve:

Arrange the sliced pork on a serving platter.

Garnish with chopped fresh cilantro and serve with pineapple slices on the side.

Enjoy the Pineapple Sriracha Grilled Pork Tenderloin with the perfect blend of sweet, spicy, and savory flavors!

Feel free to adjust the Sriracha sauce quantity according to your spice preference.

Coffee-Rubbed Grilled Ribeye

Ingredients:

For the Coffee Rub:

- 2 tablespoons finely ground coffee
- 2 tablespoons brown sugar
- 1 tablespoon smoked paprika
- 1 tablespoon chili powder
- 1 tablespoon ground coriander
- 1 tablespoon kosher salt
- 1 teaspoon black pepper
- 1 teaspoon garlic powder
- 1 teaspoon onion powder
- 1/2 teaspoon cayenne pepper (adjust to taste)

For the Ribeye:

- 2 bone-in ribeye steaks (about 1.5 inches thick)
- 2 tablespoons olive oil

Instructions:

1. Prepare the Coffee Rub:

In a small bowl, combine the finely ground coffee, brown sugar, smoked paprika, chili powder, ground coriander, kosher salt, black pepper, garlic powder, onion powder, and cayenne pepper. Mix well to create the coffee rub.

2. Prepare the Ribeye:

Preheat your grill to high heat.
Pat the ribeye steaks dry with paper towels.
Brush the steaks with olive oil to help the coffee rub adhere.

3. Apply the Coffee Rub:

Generously coat both sides of each ribeye with the coffee rub, pressing the rub into the meat to adhere.

Let the steaks sit at room temperature for about 15-20 minutes to allow the flavors to penetrate the meat.

4. Grilling the Ribeye:

Place the coffee-rubbed ribeye steaks on the preheated grill. For medium-rare, grill for about 6-7 minutes per side, adjusting the time for your preferred doneness.

Allow the steaks to rest for 5 minutes after grilling.

5. Slicing and Serving:

Slice the ribeye steaks against the grain into thick slices.

Serve the Coffee-Rubbed Grilled Ribeye hot, with your favorite side dishes.

Enjoy the rich and aromatic flavor of coffee-infused grilled ribeye!

This unique coffee rub adds depth and complexity to the ribeye, creating a delicious and memorable dining experience.

Grilled Bratwurst with Beer-Braised Onions

Ingredients:

For the Bratwurst:

- 4 bratwurst sausages
- 4 bratwurst buns

For the Beer-Braised Onions:

- 2 large onions, thinly sliced
- 2 tablespoons butter
- 1 cup beer (choose a flavorful beer, like a lager or ale)
- 1 tablespoon brown sugar
- 1 teaspoon Dijon mustard
- Salt and black pepper to taste

Optional Toppings:

- Mustard
- Sauerkraut
- Pickles

Instructions:

1. Prepare the Beer-Braised Onions:

    In a large skillet, melt the butter over medium heat.
    Add the thinly sliced onions to the skillet and cook until they become soft and caramelized, stirring occasionally.
    Pour in the beer, brown sugar, Dijon mustard, salt, and black pepper. Stir well to combine.
    Simmer the onions in the beer mixture until most of the liquid has evaporated, and the onions are tender and flavorful. This usually takes about 15-20 minutes.
    Adjust the seasoning if needed and set the beer-braised onions aside.

2. Grill the Bratwurst:

    Preheat your grill to medium-high heat.

Grill the bratwurst sausages for about 10-12 minutes, turning occasionally, or until they are browned and cooked through.
During the last few minutes of grilling, you can toast the bratwurst buns on the grill.

3. Assemble and Serve:

    Place a grilled bratwurst in each bun.
    Top the bratwurst with a generous portion of the beer-braised onions.
    Add optional toppings such as mustard, sauerkraut, or pickles according to your preference.
    Serve the Grilled Bratwurst with Beer-Braised Onions hot, and enjoy this classic and flavorful dish!

This recipe combines the smoky goodness of grilled bratwurst with the sweet and savory flavor of beer-braised onions for a delicious and satisfying meal.

Burger Creations:

Ultimate Bacon BBQ Burger

Ingredients:

For the Burger Patties:

- 1.5 lbs ground beef (80% lean)
- Salt and black pepper to taste
- 1 tablespoon Worcestershire sauce
- 1 teaspoon garlic powder
- 1 teaspoon onion powder

For the Burger Toppings:

- 8 strips of crispy bacon
- 4 slices of your favorite cheese (cheddar, Swiss, or pepper jack work well)
- 4 hamburger buns, toasted

For the BBQ Sauce:

- 1/2 cup barbecue sauce (use your favorite brand)
- 2 tablespoons ketchup
- 1 tablespoon brown sugar
- 1 tablespoon Dijon mustard

For Assembly:

- Lettuce leaves
- Sliced tomatoes
- Sliced red onions
- Pickles
- Mayonnaise and mustard for spreading

Instructions:

1. Prepare the Burger Patties:

In a bowl, combine the ground beef, salt, black pepper, Worcestershire sauce, garlic powder, and onion powder. Mix gently until just combined; avoid overmixing to keep the patties tender.
Divide the mixture into 4 equal portions and shape them into burger patties.
Preheat your grill to medium-high heat.
Grill the burger patties for about 4-5 minutes per side, or until they reach your desired level of doneness.
In the last minute of cooking, place a slice of cheese on each patty and allow it to melt.

2. Prepare the BBQ Sauce:

In a small bowl, whisk together barbecue sauce, ketchup, brown sugar, and Dijon mustard.

3. Assemble the Ultimate Bacon BBQ Burger:

Spread mayonnaise on the bottom half of each toasted bun. Place a lettuce leaf on top.
Add the grilled burger patties with melted cheese on the lettuce.
Spoon a generous amount of the BBQ sauce over the patties.
Top each patty with two strips of crispy bacon.
Add slices of tomato, red onion, and pickles.
Complete the burger with the top half of the toasted bun.

4. Serve and Enjoy:

Serve the Ultimate Bacon BBQ Burger hot, and enjoy the delicious combination of flavors and textures!

Feel free to customize the toppings and condiments according to your taste preferences.

Portobello Mushroom Veggie Burger

Ingredients:

For the Portobello Patties:

- 4 large portobello mushrooms, stems removed
- 3 tablespoons balsamic vinegar
- 2 tablespoons soy sauce
- 2 tablespoons olive oil
- 2 cloves garlic, minced
- 1 teaspoon dried thyme
- Salt and black pepper to taste

For the Burger Assembly:

- 4 whole wheat burger buns, toasted
- 1 cup baby spinach or arugula
- 1 large tomato, sliced
- 1 red onion, thinly sliced
- 4 slices Swiss or your favorite cheese
- Dijon mustard and mayonnaise for spreading

Instructions:

1. Marinate the Portobello Mushrooms:

   In a bowl, whisk together balsamic vinegar, soy sauce, olive oil, minced garlic, dried thyme, salt, and black pepper.
   Place the portobello mushrooms in a shallow dish and pour the marinade over them. Allow them to marinate for at least 30 minutes, turning occasionally to coat both sides.

2. Grill the Portobello Patties:

   Preheat your grill or grill pan to medium-high heat.
   Grill the marinated portobello mushrooms for about 4-5 minutes per side, or until they are tender and have grill marks.
   In the last minute of grilling, place a slice of Swiss cheese on each mushroom to melt.

3. Assemble the Veggie Burger:

   Spread Dijon mustard on the bottom half of each toasted bun.
   Place a grilled portobello mushroom with melted cheese on the bun.
   Top with baby spinach or arugula, tomato slices, and red onion rings.
   Spread mayonnaise on the top half of the bun and place it on top of the veggie burger.

4. Serve and Enjoy:

Serve the Portobello Mushroom Veggie Burger immediately, and enjoy this hearty and flavorful vegetarian option!

Feel free to add additional condiments or customize the toppings to suit your taste preferences.

Southwest Chipotle Turkey Burgers

Ingredients:

For the Turkey Patties:

- 1.5 lbs ground turkey
- 1/2 cup breadcrumbs
- 1/4 cup chopped fresh cilantro
- 1/4 cup finely chopped red onion
- 2 cloves garlic, minced
- 1 chipotle pepper in adobo sauce, minced (adjust to taste)
- 1 teaspoon ground cumin
- 1 teaspoon chili powder
- 1/2 teaspoon smoked paprika
- Salt and black pepper to taste

For the Chipotle Mayo:

- 1/2 cup mayonnaise
- 1 chipotle pepper in adobo sauce, minced
- 1 tablespoon lime juice
- Salt to taste

For Burger Assembly:

- Whole wheat burger buns, toasted
- Pepper jack cheese slices
- Sliced avocado
- Tomato slices
- Red onion rings
- Lettuce leaves

Instructions:

1. Prepare the Turkey Patties:

In a large bowl, combine ground turkey, breadcrumbs, chopped cilantro, chopped red onion, minced garlic, minced chipotle pepper, ground cumin, chili powder, smoked paprika, salt, and black pepper.

Mix the ingredients until well combined, but be careful not to overmix to keep the patties tender.

Divide the mixture into 4 equal portions and shape them into burger patties.

Preheat your grill to medium-high heat.

Grill the turkey patties for about 5-6 minutes per side, or until they are cooked through and have nice grill marks.

2. Prepare the Chipotle Mayo:

In a small bowl, mix together mayonnaise, minced chipotle pepper, lime juice, and salt. Adjust the seasoning to taste.

3. Assemble the Southwest Chipotle Turkey Burgers:

Spread a generous dollop of chipotle mayo on the bottom half of each toasted bun.

Place a turkey patty on the bun.

Add a slice of pepper jack cheese, followed by sliced avocado, tomato slices, red onion rings, and lettuce leaves.

Complete the burger with the top half of the toasted bun.

4. Serve and Enjoy:

Serve the Southwest Chipotle Turkey Burgers hot, and savor the bold and spicy flavors of this delicious turkey burger!

Feel free to customize the toppings or add your favorite condiments to suit your taste.

Blue Cheese-Stuffed Grilled Buffalo Chicken Burger

Ingredients:

For the Blue Cheese-Stuffed Chicken Patties:

- 1.5 lbs ground chicken
- 1/2 cup breadcrumbs
- 1/4 cup chopped green onions
- 1/4 cup crumbled blue cheese
- 1/4 cup buffalo sauce (plus extra for brushing)
- 1 teaspoon garlic powder
- Salt and black pepper to taste
- 4 ounces blue cheese, sliced (for stuffing)

For the Burger Assembly:

- Whole wheat burger buns, toasted
- Lettuce leaves
- Tomato slices
- Red onion rings
- Extra buffalo sauce for brushing
- Ranch or blue cheese dressing (optional, for drizzling)

Instructions:

1. Prepare the Blue Cheese-Stuffed Chicken Patties:

    In a large bowl, combine ground chicken, breadcrumbs, chopped green onions, crumbled blue cheese, buffalo sauce, garlic powder, salt, and black pepper.
    Mix the ingredients until well combined.
    Divide the mixture into 8 equal portions. Take each portion and flatten it into a patty shape.
    Place a slice of blue cheese in the center of 4 patties. Top each with another patty, sealing the edges to encase the blue cheese.
    Preheat your grill to medium-high heat.
    Grill the stuffed chicken patties for about 6-7 minutes per side, or until they are cooked through and have nice grill marks.
    Brush the patties with additional buffalo sauce during the last couple of minutes of grilling.

2. Assemble the Buffalo Chicken Burgers:

> Spread ranch or blue cheese dressing on the bottom half of each toasted bun.
> Place a blue cheese-stuffed chicken patty on the bun.
> Add lettuce leaves, tomato slices, and red onion rings.
> Drizzle extra buffalo sauce on top if you desire an extra kick.
> Complete the burger with the top half of the toasted bun.

3. Serve and Enjoy:

Serve the Blue Cheese-Stuffed Grilled Buffalo Chicken Burgers hot, and savor the flavorful combination of spicy buffalo sauce and creamy blue cheese!

Feel free to customize the toppings and condiments according to your taste preferences.

Hawaiian Teriyaki Pineapple Burger

Ingredients:

For the Teriyaki Pineapple Sauce:

- 1 cup teriyaki sauce
- 1/2 cup pineapple juice
- 1/4 cup brown sugar
- 2 cloves garlic, minced
- 1 teaspoon grated fresh ginger
- 1 tablespoon cornstarch mixed with 2 tablespoons water (optional, for thickening)

For the Burger Patties:

- 1.5 lbs ground beef or ground turkey
- Salt and black pepper to taste
- 4 slices of Swiss or provolone cheese
- 4 whole wheat burger buns, toasted

For Burger Assembly:

- Grilled pineapple slices
- Crispy bacon strips
- Lettuce leaves
- Red onion rings
- Teriyaki Pineapple Sauce
- Mayonnaise and mustard for spreading

Instructions:

1. Prepare the Teriyaki Pineapple Sauce:

   In a saucepan, combine teriyaki sauce, pineapple juice, brown sugar, minced garlic, and grated ginger.
   Bring the mixture to a simmer over medium heat, stirring occasionally.

If you prefer a thicker sauce, whisk in the cornstarch-water mixture and continue to simmer until the sauce thickens. Remove from heat and set aside.

2. Grill the Burger Patties:

Preheat your grill to medium-high heat.
Season the ground beef or turkey with salt and black pepper.
Shape the meat into burger patties.
Grill the patties for about 4-5 minutes per side, or until they reach your desired level of doneness.
In the last minute of grilling, place a slice of Swiss or provolone cheese on each patty and let it melt.

3. Grill Pineapple Slices and Assemble the Burgers:

While the burgers are grilling, grill pineapple slices until they have grill marks.
Spread mayonnaise on the bottom half of each toasted bun.
Place a lettuce leaf on the bun, followed by the grilled burger patty with melted cheese.
Add a grilled pineapple slice on top of the patty.
Place crispy bacon strips and red onion rings on the pineapple.
Drizzle the Teriyaki Pineapple Sauce over the burger.
Complete the burger with the top half of the toasted bun.

4. Serve and Enjoy:

Serve the Hawaiian Teriyaki Pineapple Burger hot, and enjoy the sweet and savory flavors of this tropical-inspired delight!

Feel free to customize the toppings and adjust the sauce to your taste preferences.

Greek Lamb Burgers with Tzatziki Sauce

Ingredients:

For the Lamb Burgers:

- 1.5 lbs ground lamb
- 1/2 cup breadcrumbs
- 1/4 cup crumbled feta cheese
- 1/4 cup finely chopped red onion
- 2 cloves garlic, minced
- 1 tablespoon chopped fresh mint
- 1 tablespoon chopped fresh oregano
- 1 teaspoon ground cumin
- Salt and black pepper to taste
- Olive oil for grilling

For the Tzatziki Sauce:

- 1 cup Greek yogurt
- 1/2 cucumber, peeled, seeded, and finely diced
- 2 cloves garlic, minced
- 1 tablespoon chopped fresh dill
- 1 tablespoon lemon juice
- Salt and black pepper to taste

For Burger Assembly:

- Whole wheat burger buns, toasted
- Sliced tomatoes
- Red onion rings
- Lettuce leaves

Instructions:

1. Prepare the Lamb Burgers:

In a large bowl, combine ground lamb, breadcrumbs, crumbled feta cheese, chopped red onion, minced garlic, chopped mint, chopped oregano, ground cumin, salt, and black pepper.

Mix the ingredients until well combined.

Divide the mixture into 4 equal portions and shape them into burger patties.

Preheat your grill to medium-high heat.

Brush the grill grates with olive oil to prevent sticking.

Grill the lamb burgers for about 4-5 minutes per side, or until they are cooked to your desired level of doneness.

2. Prepare the Tzatziki Sauce:

In a bowl, combine Greek yogurt, finely diced cucumber, minced garlic, chopped dill, lemon juice, salt, and black pepper.

Mix well and refrigerate until ready to use.

3. Assemble the Greek Lamb Burgers:

Spread a generous dollop of Tzatziki sauce on the bottom half of each toasted bun.

Place a lamb burger on the bun.

Top with sliced tomatoes, red onion rings, and lettuce leaves.

Complete the burger with the top half of the toasted bun.

4. Serve and Enjoy:

Serve the Greek Lamb Burgers with Tzatziki Sauce hot, and savor the Mediterranean flavors in every bite!

Feel free to customize the toppings and add kalamata olives or other Greek-inspired ingredients to enhance the experience.

Tex-Mex BBQ Black Bean Burger

Ingredients:

For the Black Bean Patties:

- 2 cans (15 oz each) black beans, drained and rinsed
- 1 cup breadcrumbs
- 1/2 cup corn kernels (fresh or frozen)
- 1/4 cup finely chopped red onion
- 1/4 cup chopped fresh cilantro
- 2 cloves garlic, minced
- 1 teaspoon ground cumin
- 1 teaspoon chili powder
- Salt and black pepper to taste
- 1 large egg (optional, for binding)
- Olive oil for grilling

For the Tex-Mex BBQ Sauce:

- 1/2 cup barbecue sauce
- 2 tablespoons diced canned green chilies
- 1 tablespoon lime juice
- 1 teaspoon ground cumin

For Burger Assembly:

- Whole wheat burger buns, toasted
- Sliced pepper jack cheese
- Avocado slices
- Tomato slices
- Red onion rings
- Lettuce leaves

Instructions:

1. Prepare the Black Bean Patties:

   In a large bowl, mash the black beans with a fork or potato masher until mostly smooth but with some chunks remaining.

Add breadcrumbs, corn kernels, chopped red onion, chopped cilantro, minced garlic, ground cumin, chili powder, salt, and black pepper to the mashed black beans.

If using, add the egg to the mixture for additional binding.

Mix the ingredients until well combined.

Divide the mixture into 4 equal portions and shape them into burger patties.

Preheat your grill to medium-high heat.

Brush the grill grates with olive oil to prevent sticking.

Grill the black bean burgers for about 4-5 minutes per side, or until they are heated through and have nice grill marks.

2. Prepare the Tex-Mex BBQ Sauce:

In a small bowl, combine barbecue sauce, diced green chilies, lime juice, and ground cumin.

Mix well to create the Tex-Mex BBQ sauce.

3. Assemble the Tex-Mex BBQ Black Bean Burger:

Spread a spoonful of Tex-Mex BBQ sauce on the bottom half of each toasted bun.

Place a black bean burger on the bun.

Top with a slice of pepper jack cheese, avocado slices, tomato slices, red onion rings, and lettuce leaves.

Complete the burger with the top half of the toasted bun.

4. Serve and Enjoy:

Serve the Tex-Mex BBQ Black Bean Burger hot, and relish the Tex-Mex and barbecue flavors combined in this delicious and hearty vegetarian option!

Feel free to customize the toppings and adjust the spice level to suit your taste.

Salmon Avocado Burger with Dill Mayo

Ingredients:

For the Salmon Patties:

- 1 lb fresh salmon fillets, skin removed
- 1/4 cup breadcrumbs
- 1/4 cup finely chopped red onion
- 2 tablespoons chopped fresh dill
- 1 tablespoon Dijon mustard
- 1 tablespoon lemon juice
- Salt and black pepper to taste
- Olive oil for grilling

For the Dill Mayo:

- 1/2 cup mayonnaise
- 1 tablespoon chopped fresh dill
- 1 teaspoon Dijon mustard
- 1 teaspoon lemon juice
- Salt and black pepper to taste

For Burger Assembly:

- Whole wheat burger buns, toasted
- Sliced avocado
- Lettuce leaves
- Tomato slices
- Red onion rings

Instructions:

1. Prepare the Salmon Patties:

    In a food processor, pulse the fresh salmon fillets until finely chopped, but not pureed.

In a bowl, combine the chopped salmon, breadcrumbs, chopped red onion, chopped dill, Dijon mustard, lemon juice, salt, and black pepper.
Mix the ingredients until well combined.
Divide the mixture into 4 equal portions and shape them into burger patties.
Preheat your grill to medium-high heat.
Brush the grill grates with olive oil to prevent sticking.
Grill the salmon patties for about 3-4 minutes per side, or until they are cooked through and have a nice sear.

2. Prepare the Dill Mayo:

In a small bowl, combine mayonnaise, chopped dill, Dijon mustard, lemon juice, salt, and black pepper.
Mix well to create the dill mayo.

3. Assemble the Salmon Avocado Burger:

Spread a generous dollop of dill mayo on the bottom half of each toasted bun.
Place a grilled salmon patty on the bun.
Top with sliced avocado, lettuce leaves, tomato slices, and red onion rings.
Complete the burger with the top half of the toasted bun.

4. Serve and Enjoy:

Serve the Salmon Avocado Burger with Dill Mayo hot, and savor the fresh and savory combination of salmon and creamy avocado!

Feel free to customize the toppings and add your favorite condiments to enhance the flavors.

Pesto Caprese Chicken Burger

Ingredients:

For the Chicken Patties:

- 1.5 lbs ground chicken
- 1/2 cup breadcrumbs
- 1/4 cup grated Parmesan cheese
- 2 cloves garlic, minced
- 2 tablespoons chopped fresh basil
- 1 tablespoon chopped fresh parsley
- Salt and black pepper to taste
- Olive oil for grilling

For the Pesto:

- 1 cup fresh basil leaves
- 1/3 cup grated Parmesan cheese
- 1/4 cup pine nuts
- 2 cloves garlic, minced
- 1/2 cup extra-virgin olive oil
- Salt and black pepper to taste

For Burger Assembly:

- Whole wheat burger buns, toasted
- Fresh mozzarella cheese slices
- Tomato slices
- Fresh basil leaves

Instructions:

1. Prepare the Chicken Patties:

    In a large bowl, combine ground chicken, breadcrumbs, grated Parmesan cheese, minced garlic, chopped basil, chopped parsley, salt, and black pepper.
    Mix the ingredients until well combined.

Divide the mixture into 4 equal portions and shape them into burger patties.
Preheat your grill to medium-high heat.
Brush the grill grates with olive oil to prevent sticking.
Grill the chicken patties for about 5-6 minutes per side, or until they are cooked through and have a golden brown exterior.

2. Prepare the Pesto:

In a food processor, combine fresh basil leaves, grated Parmesan cheese, pine nuts, and minced garlic.
Pulse the ingredients until finely chopped.
With the food processor running, slowly drizzle in the olive oil until the pesto reaches a smooth consistency.
Season with salt and black pepper to taste.

3. Assemble the Pesto Caprese Chicken Burger:

Spread a generous amount of pesto on the bottom half of each toasted bun.
Place a grilled chicken patty on the bun.
Top with a slice of fresh mozzarella cheese, tomato slices, and fresh basil leaves.
Complete the burger with the top half of the toasted bun.

4. Serve and Enjoy:

Serve the Pesto Caprese Chicken Burger hot, and enjoy the delightful combination of fresh flavors and vibrant pesto!

Feel free to customize the toppings and add balsamic glaze for an extra burst of flavor.

BBQ Pulled Pork Sliders

Ingredients:

For the Pulled Pork:

- 2 lbs pork shoulder or pork butt, trimmed of excess fat
- 1 tablespoon olive oil
- 1 onion, finely chopped
- 3 cloves garlic, minced
- 1 cup barbecue sauce (plus extra for serving)
- 1 cup chicken or vegetable broth
- 1 tablespoon brown sugar
- 1 tablespoon Worcestershire sauce
- 1 teaspoon smoked paprika
- Salt and black pepper to taste

For the Sliders:

- Slider buns, split and toasted
- Coleslaw (optional, for serving)
- Pickles (optional, for serving)

Instructions:

1. Prepare the Pulled Pork:

    Season the pork shoulder with salt and black pepper.
    In a large skillet or Dutch oven, heat olive oil over medium-high heat. Sear the pork on all sides until browned.
    Remove the pork from the skillet and set it aside.
    In the same skillet, add chopped onion and garlic. Cook until softened.
    Add barbecue sauce, chicken or vegetable broth, brown sugar, Worcestershire sauce, and smoked paprika to the skillet. Stir to combine.
    Return the seared pork to the skillet. Cover and simmer over low heat for 4-6 hours or until the pork is tender and easily shreds with a fork.
    Once cooked, shred the pork using two forks and mix it with the sauce in the skillet.

2. Assemble the Sliders:

>Toast the slider buns in the oven or on a grill.
>Spoon a generous portion of the pulled pork onto the bottom half of each slider bun.
>Top the pulled pork with coleslaw and pickles if desired.
>Place the top half of the slider bun on the toppings.

3. Serve and Enjoy:

Serve the BBQ Pulled Pork Sliders hot, and enjoy the savory and flavorful combination of tender pulled pork, barbecue sauce, and optional toppings!

These sliders are perfect for parties or casual gatherings, and you can customize them with your favorite coleslaw or pickles.

Grilled Vegetables:

Balsamic Glazed Grilled Vegetables

Ingredients:

For the Balsamic Glaze:

- 1/2 cup balsamic vinegar
- 2 tablespoons honey or maple syrup
- 2 cloves garlic, minced
- 1 teaspoon Dijon mustard
- Salt and black pepper to taste

For the Grilled Vegetables:

- Assorted vegetables (e.g., bell peppers, zucchini, cherry tomatoes, red onion, mushrooms, asparagus)
- 2 tablespoons olive oil
- Salt and black pepper to taste
- Fresh herbs (optional, for garnish)

Instructions:

1. Prepare the Balsamic Glaze:

    In a small saucepan, combine balsamic vinegar, honey or maple syrup, minced garlic, Dijon mustard, salt, and black pepper.
    Bring the mixture to a simmer over medium heat.
    Reduce the heat and let it simmer for 8-10 minutes or until the glaze has thickened slightly.
    Remove from heat and set aside.

2. Prepare the Grilled Vegetables:

    Preheat your grill to medium-high heat.
    Cut the vegetables into bite-sized pieces, making sure they are of similar size for even cooking.
    In a large bowl, toss the vegetables with olive oil, salt, and black pepper to coat them evenly.

Place the vegetables on the preheated grill and cook for about 8-10 minutes, turning occasionally, or until they are tender and have grill marks.

3. Glaze the Grilled Vegetables:

During the last few minutes of grilling, brush the balsamic glaze onto the vegetables, turning them to coat evenly.
Remove the vegetables from the grill once they are glazed and caramelized to your liking.

4. Serve and Garnish:

Transfer the glazed grilled vegetables to a serving platter.
Garnish with fresh herbs such as basil, thyme, or parsley if desired.

5. Enjoy:

Serve the Balsamic Glazed Grilled Vegetables as a side dish or as a flavorful addition to salads, pasta, or rice. These vegetables are a versatile and tasty option for a variety of meals.

Grilled Zucchini Ribbons with Parmesan

Ingredients:

- 3 medium-sized zucchini
- 2 tablespoons olive oil
- Salt and black pepper to taste
- 1/4 cup freshly grated Parmesan cheese
- Fresh basil or parsley, chopped (for garnish)

Instructions:

1. Prepare the Zucchini:

   Preheat your grill to medium-high heat.
   Wash and trim the ends of the zucchini.
   Using a vegetable peeler or a mandoline, slice the zucchini into thin, long ribbons.

2. Grill the Zucchini Ribbons:

   In a large bowl, toss the zucchini ribbons with olive oil, salt, and black pepper until they are evenly coated.
   Place the zucchini ribbons on the preheated grill.
   Grill for 1-2 minutes per side, or until they have grill marks and are just tender.
   Be attentive, as zucchini ribbons cook quickly, and you want to avoid overcooking.

3. Garnish and Serve:

   Transfer the grilled zucchini ribbons to a serving platter.
   Sprinkle freshly grated Parmesan cheese over the top while the zucchini is still warm.
   Garnish with chopped fresh basil or parsley for added flavor and freshness.

4. Enjoy:

Serve the Grilled Zucchini Ribbons with Parmesan as a tasty side dish or a light and healthy appetizer. They make a delightful addition to summer meals and pair well with various grilled dishes.

Cajun Spiced Grilled Corn on the Cob

Ingredients:

- 4 ears of fresh corn, husks removed
- 2 tablespoons olive oil
- 1 teaspoon paprika
- 1 teaspoon garlic powder
- 1 teaspoon onion powder
- 1/2 teaspoon thyme
- 1/2 teaspoon oregano
- 1/2 teaspoon cayenne pepper (adjust to taste)
- Salt and black pepper to taste
- Fresh cilantro or parsley, chopped (for garnish)
- Lime wedges (for serving)

Instructions:

1. Preheat the Grill:

Preheat your grill to medium-high heat.

2. Prepare the Cajun Spice Mix:

In a small bowl, mix together the paprika, garlic powder, onion powder, thyme, oregano, cayenne pepper, salt, and black pepper. This is your Cajun spice mix.

3. Grill the Corn:

>Brush each ear of corn with olive oil to coat them evenly.
>Sprinkle the Cajun spice mix over the corn, rolling and pressing so that the spices adhere to the surface.
>Place the corn on the preheated grill.
>Grill for about 10-15 minutes, turning occasionally, until the corn is tender and has a nice char.

4. Garnish and Serve:

>Remove the grilled corn from the grill and place it on a serving platter.
>Sprinkle chopped cilantro or parsley over the top for freshness.

Serve the Cajun Spiced Grilled Corn on the Cob hot with lime wedges on the side.

5. Enjoy:

Enjoy the Cajun spiced flavor and smokiness of the grilled corn. This dish is perfect for summer cookouts and pairs well with a variety of grilled meats.

Mediterranean Grilled Eggplant

Ingredients:

- 2 medium-sized eggplants, sliced into 1/2-inch rounds
- 1/4 cup olive oil
- 2 tablespoons balsamic vinegar
- 3 cloves garlic, minced
- 1 teaspoon dried oregano
- 1 teaspoon dried thyme
- Salt and black pepper to taste
- Fresh parsley, chopped (for garnish)
- Feta cheese (optional, for serving)

Instructions:

1. Preheat the Grill:

Preheat your grill to medium-high heat.

2. Prepare the Marinade:

In a small bowl, whisk together the olive oil, balsamic vinegar, minced garlic, dried oregano, dried thyme, salt, and black pepper.

3. Grill the Eggplant:

    Brush both sides of the eggplant slices with the marinade.
    Place the eggplant slices on the preheated grill.
    Grill for about 3-4 minutes per side or until they are tender and have grill marks.

4. Garnish and Serve:

    Remove the grilled eggplant from the grill and place them on a serving platter.
    Drizzle any remaining marinade over the grilled eggplant.
    Sprinkle chopped fresh parsley over the top for added flavor and freshness.
    Optionally, crumble feta cheese on top before serving.

5. Enjoy:

Serve the Mediterranean Grilled Eggplant as a tasty side dish or appetizer. This dish is full of Mediterranean flavors and can be enjoyed on its own or as part of a mezze platter.

Honey Sriracha Grilled Brussels Sprouts

Ingredients:

- 1 lb Brussels sprouts, trimmed and halved
- 2 tablespoons olive oil
- 2 tablespoons honey
- 1 tablespoon Sriracha sauce (adjust to taste)
- 2 cloves garlic, minced
- 1 tablespoon soy sauce
- Salt and black pepper to taste
- Sesame seeds (optional, for garnish)
- Chopped green onions (optional, for garnish)

Instructions:

1. Preheat the Grill:

Preheat your grill to medium-high heat.

2. Prepare the Marinade:

In a bowl, whisk together the olive oil, honey, Sriracha sauce, minced garlic, soy sauce, salt, and black pepper. This is your marinade.

3. Grill the Brussels Sprouts:

> Toss the halved Brussels sprouts in the marinade until they are well coated.
> Thread the Brussels sprouts onto skewers or place them directly on the grill grates.
> Grill for about 8-10 minutes, turning occasionally, or until the Brussels sprouts are tender and have a nice char.

4. Garnish and Serve:

> Remove the grilled Brussels sprouts from the grill and place them on a serving platter.

Optionally, sprinkle sesame seeds and chopped green onions over the top for garnish.

5. Enjoy:

Serve the Honey Sriracha Grilled Brussels Sprouts as a flavorful side dish or appetizer. The sweet and spicy glaze enhances the natural flavors of the Brussels sprouts, making them a delicious addition to any meal.

Grilled Asparagus with Lemon Zest

Ingredients:

- 1 lb fresh asparagus, trimmed
- 2 tablespoons olive oil
- Zest of 1 lemon
- Salt and black pepper to taste
- Lemon wedges (for serving)

Instructions:

1. Preheat the Grill:

Preheat your grill to medium-high heat.

2. Prepare the Asparagus:

Trim the tough ends of the asparagus spears.
In a large bowl, toss the asparagus with olive oil until evenly coated.

3. Grill the Asparagus:

Place the asparagus spears on the preheated grill.
Grill for about 4-6 minutes, turning occasionally, or until the asparagus is tender and has a slight char.

4. Zest and Season:

Once the asparagus is grilled, transfer it to a serving platter.
Zest the lemon directly over the grilled asparagus.
Sprinkle salt and black pepper over the asparagus to taste.

5. Serve:

Serve the Grilled Asparagus with Lemon Zest hot, and squeeze fresh lemon wedges over the top just before serving for an extra burst of citrus flavor.

Enjoy this simple and refreshing side dish that highlights the natural goodness of asparagus with the zesty brightness of lemon.

Mexican Street Corn (Elote)

Ingredients:

- 4-6 ears of fresh corn, husks removed
- 1/2 cup mayonnaise
- 1/2 cup sour cream
- 1 cup crumbled cotija cheese (or feta cheese)
- 1 teaspoon chili powder (adjust to taste)
- 1/2 teaspoon smoked paprika
- 1/4 cup chopped fresh cilantro
- 1 lime, cut into wedges

Instructions:

1. Preheat the Grill:

Preheat your grill to medium-high heat.

2. Grill the Corn:

   Place the corn directly on the preheated grill.
   Grill for about 10-12 minutes, turning occasionally, or until the corn has a nice char and is cooked through.

3. Prepare the Sauce:

   In a bowl, mix together mayonnaise and sour cream.
   In a separate shallow dish, combine crumbled cotija cheese, chili powder, and smoked paprika.

4. Coat the Corn:

   Once the corn is grilled, brush each ear with the mayonnaise-sour cream mixture.
   Roll the coated corn in the cotija cheese and spice mixture, ensuring an even coating.

5. Garnish and Serve:

   Place the coated corn on a serving platter.
   Sprinkle chopped cilantro over the top.

Serve the Mexican Street Corn hot with lime wedges on the side.

6. Enjoy:

Enjoy the delicious flavors of Mexican Street Corn, a perfect combination of smoky, creamy, and tangy elements. This classic street food is sure to be a hit at your next barbecue or gathering.

Herb-Marinated Grilled Portobello Mushrooms

Ingredients:

- 4 large Portobello mushrooms, stems removed
- 1/4 cup balsamic vinegar
- 1/4 cup olive oil
- 2 cloves garlic, minced
- 1 tablespoon Dijon mustard
- 1 tablespoon chopped fresh thyme
- 1 tablespoon chopped fresh rosemary
- Salt and black pepper to taste
- Fresh parsley, chopped (for garnish)

Instructions:

1. Prepare the Marinade:

In a bowl, whisk together balsamic vinegar, olive oil, minced garlic, Dijon mustard, chopped thyme, chopped rosemary, salt, and black pepper. This is your herb marinade.

2. Marinate the Portobello Mushrooms:

Place the Portobello mushrooms in a shallow dish, gill side up.
Pour the herb marinade over the mushrooms, ensuring they are well-coated. Let them marinate for at least 30 minutes, allowing the flavors to infuse.

3. Preheat the Grill:

Preheat your grill to medium-high heat.

4. Grill the Portobello Mushrooms:

Place the marinated Portobello mushrooms on the preheated grill, gill side down.

Grill for about 4-5 minutes per side, or until they are tender and have grill marks.

5. Garnish and Serve:

    Transfer the grilled Portobello mushrooms to a serving platter.
    Sprinkle chopped fresh parsley over the top for garnish.

6. Enjoy:

Serve the Herb-Marinated Grilled Portobello Mushrooms as a flavorful side dish, on top of a salad, or as a meaty and satisfying vegetarian option. The combination of balsamic, herbs, and grilled mushrooms creates a delicious and savory dish.

Grilled Sweet Potato Wedges

Ingredients:

- 2 large sweet potatoes, washed and scrubbed
- 2 tablespoons olive oil
- 1 teaspoon smoked paprika
- 1 teaspoon garlic powder
- 1 teaspoon ground cumin
- Salt and black pepper to taste
- Fresh parsley, chopped (for garnish)

Instructions:

1. Preheat the Grill:

Preheat your grill to medium-high heat.

2. Prepare the Sweet Potatoes:

Cut the sweet potatoes into wedges. You can leave the skin on for added texture. In a bowl, toss the sweet potato wedges with olive oil, smoked paprika, garlic powder, ground cumin, salt, and black pepper until evenly coated.

3. Grill the Sweet Potato Wedges:

Place the seasoned sweet potato wedges directly on the preheated grill.
Grill for about 15-20 minutes, turning occasionally, or until the sweet potatoes are tender and have grill marks.

4. Garnish and Serve:

Remove the grilled sweet potato wedges from the grill and place them on a serving platter.
Sprinkle chopped fresh parsley over the top for garnish.

5. Enjoy:

Serve the Grilled Sweet Potato Wedges hot as a tasty and nutritious side dish. The smokiness from the grill combined with the seasonings makes these wedges a delightful addition to your barbecue or as a standalone snack.

Teriyaki Glazed Grilled Pineapple

Ingredients:

- 1 whole pineapple, peeled, cored, and sliced into rings or wedges
- 1/2 cup teriyaki sauce
- 2 tablespoons honey
- 1 tablespoon sesame oil
- 1 teaspoon grated fresh ginger
- 1 teaspoon garlic powder
- Sesame seeds (for garnish, optional)
- Fresh mint or cilantro (for garnish, optional)
- Vanilla ice cream (optional, for serving)

Instructions:

1. Preheat the Grill:

Preheat your grill to medium-high heat.

2. Prepare the Teriyaki Glaze:

In a bowl, whisk together teriyaki sauce, honey, sesame oil, grated ginger, and garlic powder. This is your teriyaki glaze.

3. Grill the Pineapple:

Brush the pineapple slices with the teriyaki glaze, ensuring they are well-coated.
Place the pineapple slices directly on the preheated grill.
Grill for about 2-3 minutes per side, or until they have nice grill marks and are slightly caramelized.

4. Garnish and Serve:

Remove the grilled pineapple from the grill and place them on a serving platter.
Drizzle any remaining teriyaki glaze over the grilled pineapple.
Optionally, sprinkle sesame seeds and fresh mint or cilantro over the top for garnish.

5. Optional Serving:

Serve the Teriyaki Glazed Grilled Pineapple on its own as a refreshing dessert, or pair it with a scoop of vanilla ice cream for an extra treat.

6. Enjoy:

Enjoy the sweet and savory combination of teriyaki-glazed grilled pineapple – a delightful and easy-to-make dessert that's perfect for summer gatherings!

Seafood Delights:

Grilled Lobster Tails with Garlic Butter

Ingredients:

- 4 lobster tails, thawed if frozen
- 1/2 cup unsalted butter, melted
- 4 cloves garlic, minced
- 1 tablespoon fresh lemon juice
- 1 tablespoon chopped fresh parsley
- Salt and black pepper to taste
- Lemon wedges (for serving)

Instructions:

1. Preheat the Grill:

Preheat your grill to medium-high heat.

2. Prepare the Garlic Butter Sauce:

In a small saucepan over medium heat, melt the butter.
Add minced garlic to the melted butter and sauté for 1-2 minutes until fragrant.
Remove the saucepan from heat and stir in fresh lemon juice, chopped parsley, salt, and black pepper. This is your garlic butter sauce.

3. Prep the Lobster Tails:

Use kitchen shears to cut the top of the lobster shells lengthwise, exposing the meat.
Gently pull the lobster meat slightly from the shell, leaving it attached at the bottom.

4. Grill the Lobster Tails:

Brush the lobster tails with the prepared garlic butter sauce, ensuring they are well-coated.
Place the lobster tails on the preheated grill, shell side down.
Grill for about 5-7 minutes, basting occasionally with more garlic butter sauce, or until the lobster meat is opaque and cooked through.

5. Serve:

Remove the grilled lobster tails from the grill and place them on a serving platter.
Drizzle with any remaining garlic butter sauce.
Serve hot with lemon wedges on the side.

6. Enjoy:

Enjoy these Grilled Lobster Tails with Garlic Butter as a luxurious and flavorful dish. The combination of smoky grilled flavor and rich garlic butter enhances the natural sweetness of the lobster meat.

Tequila Lime Grilled Shrimp Tacos

Ingredients:

For the Tequila Lime Marinade:

- 1/4 cup tequila
- 1/4 cup fresh lime juice
- 2 tablespoons olive oil
- 2 cloves garlic, minced
- 1 teaspoon ground cumin
- 1 teaspoon chili powder
- Salt and black pepper to taste

For the Grilled Shrimp:

- 1 lb large shrimp, peeled and deveined
- Tequila Lime Marinade

For Taco Assembly:

- Corn or flour tortillas
- Shredded cabbage or lettuce
- Diced tomatoes
- Red onion, thinly sliced
- Fresh cilantro, chopped
- Avocado slices
- Lime wedges
- Sour cream or your favorite sauce (optional)

Instructions:

1. Prepare the Tequila Lime Marinade:

In a bowl, whisk together tequila, fresh lime juice, olive oil, minced garlic, ground cumin, chili powder, salt, and black pepper to create the marinade.

2. Marinate the Shrimp:

Place the peeled and deveined shrimp in a resealable plastic bag or shallow dish. Pour the Tequila Lime Marinade over the shrimp, making sure they are well-coated. Marinate in the refrigerator for at least 30 minutes.

3. Grill the Shrimp:

Preheat your grill to medium-high heat.

Thread the marinated shrimp onto skewers or use a grilling basket. Grill for 2-3 minutes per side or until the shrimp are opaque and have grill marks.

4. Assemble the Tacos:

> Warm the tortillas on the grill or in a dry skillet.
> Place a portion of grilled shrimp on each tortilla.
> Top with shredded cabbage or lettuce, diced tomatoes, red onion slices, chopped cilantro, and avocado slices.

5. Serve:

Serve the Tequila Lime Grilled Shrimp Tacos with lime wedges and optional sour cream or your favorite sauce.

6. Enjoy:

Enjoy these flavorful and zesty tacos that showcase the delicious combination of tequila and lime with perfectly grilled shrimp!

Citrus-Marinated Grilled Swordfish

Ingredients:

For the Citrus Marinade:

- 1/4 cup fresh orange juice
- 1/4 cup fresh lemon juice
- 2 tablespoons fresh lime juice
- 1/4 cup olive oil
- 2 cloves garlic, minced
- 1 teaspoon dried oregano
- 1 teaspoon ground cumin
- Salt and black pepper to taste

For the Swordfish:

- 4 swordfish steaks (about 6 ounces each)
- Citrus Marinade

Instructions:

1. Prepare the Citrus Marinade:

In a bowl, whisk together fresh orange juice, fresh lemon juice, fresh lime juice, olive oil, minced garlic, dried oregano, ground cumin, salt, and black pepper. This is your citrus marinade.

2. Marinate the Swordfish:

Place the swordfish steaks in a shallow dish or a resealable plastic bag. Pour the Citrus Marinade over the swordfish, making sure each steak is well-coated. Marinate in the refrigerator for at least 30 minutes.

3. Preheat the Grill:

Preheat your grill to medium-high heat.

4. Grill the Swordfish:

> Remove the swordfish steaks from the marinade and let any excess marinade drip off.
> Place the swordfish steaks on the preheated grill.
> Grill for about 4-5 minutes per side, or until the swordfish is cooked through and has grill marks.

5. Serve:

Serve the Citrus-Marinated Grilled Swordfish hot, garnished with additional fresh citrus slices if desired.

6. Enjoy:

Enjoy this flavorful and light dish that highlights the natural taste of swordfish complemented by the citrusy and herby marinade. It pairs well with your favorite side dishes and makes for a delightful summertime meal.

Grilled Scallop Skewers with Lemon-Herb Drizzle

Ingredients:

For the Scallop Skewers:

- 1 lb large sea scallops, cleaned
- 2 tablespoons olive oil
- Salt and black pepper to taste
- Wooden or metal skewers (if using wooden skewers, soak them in water for 30 minutes)

For the Lemon-Herb Drizzle:

- 1/4 cup olive oil
- Zest of 1 lemon
- 2 tablespoons fresh lemon juice
- 2 tablespoons chopped fresh herbs (such as parsley, chives, or cilantro)
- 1 clove garlic, minced
- Salt and black pepper to taste

Instructions:

1. Preheat the Grill:

Preheat your grill to medium-high heat.

2. Prepare the Scallop Skewers:

In a bowl, toss the sea scallops with olive oil, salt, and black pepper until evenly coated.
Thread the scallops onto skewers, leaving space between each scallop.

3. Grill the Scallop Skewers:

Place the skewers on the preheated grill.

Grill for about 2-3 minutes per side, or until the scallops are opaque and have grill marks.

4. Prepare the Lemon-Herb Drizzle:

In a small bowl, whisk together olive oil, lemon zest, fresh lemon juice, chopped fresh herbs, minced garlic, salt, and black pepper. This is your lemon-herb drizzle.

5. Serve:

Remove the grilled scallop skewers from the grill and place them on a serving platter. Drizzle the lemon-herb mixture over the top.

6. Enjoy:

Serve the Grilled Scallop Skewers with Lemon-Herb Drizzle hot, and enjoy the succulent flavor of perfectly grilled scallops with the bright and herby drizzle. It's a delightful appetizer or main dish for a special occasion.

Cajun Grilled Catfish Fillets

Ingredients:

For the Cajun Spice Rub:

- 1 tablespoon paprika
- 1 teaspoon onion powder
- 1 teaspoon garlic powder
- 1 teaspoon dried thyme
- 1 teaspoon dried oregano
- 1/2 teaspoon cayenne pepper (adjust to taste)
- 1/2 teaspoon black pepper
- 1/2 teaspoon white pepper
- 1/2 teaspoon smoked paprika
- Salt to taste

For the Catfish:

- 4 catfish fillets (about 6-8 ounces each)
- 2 tablespoons olive oil
- Cajun Spice Rub

Instructions:

1. Preheat the Grill:

Preheat your grill to medium-high heat.

2. Prepare the Cajun Spice Rub:

In a bowl, mix together paprika, onion powder, garlic powder, dried thyme, dried oregano, cayenne pepper, black pepper, white pepper, smoked paprika, and salt. This is your Cajun spice rub.

3. Season the Catfish:

Pat the catfish fillets dry with paper towels.
Rub each fillet with olive oil, ensuring they are well-coated.
Sprinkle the Cajun spice rub over both sides of each catfish fillet, pressing the spices into the flesh.

4. Grill the Catfish:

Place the seasoned catfish fillets on the preheated grill.
Grill for about 4-5 minutes per side, or until the catfish is opaque and easily flakes with a fork.

5. Serve:

Remove the grilled Cajun catfish fillets from the grill and place them on a serving platter.

6. Enjoy:

Serve the Cajun Grilled Catfish Fillets hot, and enjoy the bold and spicy flavors of this Cajun-inspired dish. It pairs well with rice, vegetables, or a refreshing side salad.

Chimichurri Grilled Octopus

Ingredients:

For the Grilled Octopus:

- 2 lbs octopus, cleaned and tentacles separated
- 2 tablespoons olive oil
- Salt and black pepper to taste

For the Chimichurri Sauce:

- 1 cup fresh parsley, finely chopped
- 1/4 cup fresh cilantro, finely chopped
- 4 cloves garlic, minced
- 1 teaspoon dried oregano
- 1 teaspoon red pepper flakes (adjust to taste)
- 1/2 cup extra-virgin olive oil
- 3 tablespoons red wine vinegar
- Salt and black pepper to taste

Instructions:

1. Prepare the Octopus:

   Preheat your grill to medium-high heat.
   Rinse the octopus under cold water and pat it dry with paper towels.
   In a bowl, toss the octopus tentacles with olive oil, salt, and black pepper until well-coated.

2. Grill the Octopus:

   Place the octopus tentacles on the preheated grill.
   Grill for about 3-4 minutes per side, or until the octopus is cooked through and has a nice char.

3. Prepare the Chimichurri Sauce:

In a bowl, combine finely chopped fresh parsley, finely chopped fresh cilantro, minced garlic, dried oregano, red pepper flakes, extra-virgin olive oil, red wine vinegar, salt, and black pepper. Mix well to create the chimichurri sauce.

4. Serve:

Remove the grilled octopus from the grill and place it on a serving platter. Drizzle the chimichurri sauce over the grilled octopus or serve it on the side.

5. Enjoy:

Serve the Chimichurri Grilled Octopus hot, and savor the delightful combination of tender octopus with the bold and herby flavors of chimichurri. It makes for a unique and delicious seafood dish.

Thai Coconut Lemongrass Grilled Mussels

Ingredients:

For the Coconut Lemongrass Sauce:

- 1 can (14 oz) coconut milk
- 2 tablespoons Thai red curry paste
- 2 tablespoons fish sauce
- 2 tablespoons soy sauce
- 2 tablespoons brown sugar
- 2 stalks lemongrass, bruised and chopped
- 3 kaffir lime leaves, torn into pieces (optional)
- Zest of 1 lime
- Juice of 1 lime

For the Grilled Mussels:

- 2 lbs fresh mussels, cleaned and debearded
- 2 tablespoons vegetable oil
- Fresh cilantro, chopped (for garnish)
- Red chili slices (for garnish, optional)
- Lime wedges (for serving)

Instructions:

1. Prepare the Coconut Lemongrass Sauce:

   In a saucepan, combine coconut milk, Thai red curry paste, fish sauce, soy sauce, brown sugar, lemongrass, kaffir lime leaves (if using), lime zest, and lime juice. Bring the sauce to a gentle simmer over medium heat, stirring occasionally. Let it simmer for about 5-7 minutes to allow the flavors to meld. Remove from heat and set aside.

2. Grill the Mussels:

   Preheat your grill to medium-high heat.
   In a large bowl, toss the cleaned and debearded mussels with vegetable oil.

Place the mussels on the preheated grill. Grill for about 3-5 minutes or until the mussels open.

3. Combine and Serve:

Transfer the grilled mussels to a serving platter.
Pour the prepared Coconut Lemongrass Sauce over the grilled mussels.
Garnish with chopped cilantro and red chili slices if desired.
Serve hot with lime wedges on the side.

4. Enjoy:

Savor the rich and aromatic flavors of Thai Coconut Lemongrass Grilled Mussels. This dish is perfect for a seafood feast or a special occasion, bringing a taste of Thai cuisine to your table.

Grilled Oysters with Garlic Parmesan Butter

Ingredients:

For the Garlic Parmesan Butter:

- 1/2 cup unsalted butter, softened
- 4 cloves garlic, minced
- 1/4 cup fresh parsley, finely chopped
- 1/2 cup grated Parmesan cheese
- 1 tablespoon lemon juice
- Salt and black pepper to taste

For the Grilled Oysters:

- 2 dozen fresh oysters, in the shell
- Rock salt (for stabilizing the oysters on the grill)

Instructions:

1. Prepare the Garlic Parmesan Butter:

    In a bowl, mix together softened butter, minced garlic, finely chopped fresh parsley, grated Parmesan cheese, lemon juice, salt, and black pepper. This is your garlic Parmesan butter.
    Place the butter mixture on a piece of plastic wrap, shape it into a log or a roll, and refrigerate until firm.

2. Shuck the Oysters:

    Shuck the oysters, discarding the top shell and loosening the oyster from the bottom shell.
    Place the shucked oysters on a bed of rock salt on a baking sheet to stabilize them.

3. Grill the Oysters:

    Preheat your grill to medium-high heat.

Place the oysters on the preheated grill, making sure they are level on the rock salt.
Grill for about 4-6 minutes or until the oyster edges start to curl and the oysters are cooked through.

4. Add the Garlic Parmesan Butter:

Remove the oysters from the grill.
Slice thin rounds of the garlic Parmesan butter and place a slice on top of each hot oyster.
Let the butter melt over the oysters.

5. Serve:

Transfer the Grilled Oysters with Garlic Parmesan Butter to a serving platter.

6. Enjoy:

Serve hot and enjoy the succulent flavor of grilled oysters enhanced by the rich and savory garlic Parmesan butter. This dish is perfect for seafood lovers and makes a delightful appetizer for any occasion.

Grilled Clams with White Wine and Garlic

Ingredients:

- 2 dozen fresh clams, scrubbed and cleaned
- 2 tablespoons olive oil
- 4 cloves garlic, minced
- 1/2 cup dry white wine
- 2 tablespoons fresh parsley, chopped
- Salt and black pepper to taste
- Red pepper flakes (optional, for some heat)
- Lemon wedges (for serving)

Instructions:

1. Prepare the Clams:

    Rinse the clams under cold water to remove any sand or debris.
    Scrub the clam shells with a brush.

2. Prepare the Grilling Mixture:

    In a bowl, mix together olive oil, minced garlic, chopped fresh parsley, salt, black pepper, and red pepper flakes if you want some heat.
    Add the white wine to the mixture and stir well.

3. Grill the Clams:

    Preheat your grill to medium-high heat.
    Place the cleaned clams on the preheated grill grates.
    Spoon the olive oil, garlic, and wine mixture over the clams.
    Grill for about 5-7 minutes or until the clam shells open, and the clams are cooked through.

4. Serve:

    Remove the grilled clams from the grill and transfer them to a serving platter.
    Pour any remaining garlic and wine mixture over the top.

5. Enjoy:

Serve the Grilled Clams with White Wine and Garlic hot, with lemon wedges on the side for squeezing over the clams. This dish is perfect as an appetizer or part of a seafood feast.

Grilled Teriyaki Tuna Steaks

Ingredients:

For the Teriyaki Marinade:

- 1/4 cup soy sauce
- 2 tablespoons mirin (Japanese sweet rice wine)
- 2 tablespoons sake or dry white wine
- 2 tablespoons honey or brown sugar
- 1 tablespoon sesame oil
- 2 cloves garlic, minced
- 1 teaspoon grated fresh ginger
- 1 tablespoon chopped green onions (optional)
- 4 tuna steaks (about 6 ounces each)
- Sesame seeds and chopped green onions for garnish (optional)

Instructions:

1. Prepare the Teriyaki Marinade:

    In a bowl, whisk together soy sauce, mirin, sake, honey, sesame oil, minced garlic, grated ginger, and chopped green onions (if using).
    Reserve a portion of the marinade for basting during grilling.

2. Marinate the Tuna Steaks:

    Place the tuna steaks in a shallow dish or a resealable plastic bag.
    Pour the teriyaki marinade over the tuna steaks, ensuring they are well-coated.
    Marinate in the refrigerator for at least 30 minutes, allowing the flavors to infuse.

3. Preheat the Grill:

Preheat your grill to medium-high heat.

4. Grill the Tuna Steaks:

Remove the tuna steaks from the marinade and let any excess drip off.
Place the tuna steaks on the preheated grill.
Grill for about 2-3 minutes per side for medium-rare, or adjust the time to your desired level of doneness.
Baste the tuna with the reserved teriyaki marinade during grilling.

5. Garnish and Serve:

Remove the grilled tuna steaks from the grill and place them on a serving platter.
Garnish with sesame seeds and chopped green onions if desired.

6. Enjoy:

Serve the Grilled Teriyaki Tuna Steaks hot, and enjoy the savory and sweet flavors of the teriyaki marinade with perfectly grilled tuna. This dish pairs well with rice or a side of grilled vegetables.

Side and Accompaniments:

Grilled Caesar Salad with Homemade Croutons

Ingredients:

For the Grilled Caesar Salad:

- 2 heads of romaine lettuce, halved lengthwise
- Olive oil for brushing
- Salt and black pepper to taste
- Grated Parmesan cheese for topping

For the Caesar Dressing:

- 1/2 cup mayonnaise
- 1/4 cup grated Parmesan cheese
- 2 tablespoons Dijon mustard
- 2 tablespoons fresh lemon juice
- 2 cloves garlic, minced
- 1 teaspoon Worcestershire sauce
- Salt and black pepper to taste

For the Homemade Croutons:

- 4 cups bread cubes (from day-old bread)
- 3 tablespoons olive oil
- 1 teaspoon garlic powder
- 1 teaspoon dried oregano
- 1 teaspoon dried thyme
- Salt and black pepper to taste

Instructions:

1. Prepare the Homemade Croutons:

    Preheat your oven to 375°F (190°C).
    In a bowl, toss the bread cubes with olive oil, garlic powder, dried oregano, dried thyme, salt, and black pepper until well-coated.
    Spread the seasoned bread cubes on a baking sheet in a single layer.

Bake in the preheated oven for about 10-15 minutes or until the croutons are golden and crispy. Stir them occasionally for even toasting.

2. Make the Caesar Dressing:

In a bowl, whisk together mayonnaise, grated Parmesan cheese, Dijon mustard, fresh lemon juice, minced garlic, Worcestershire sauce, salt, and black pepper until well combined.
Adjust the seasoning to taste.

3. Grill the Romaine Lettuce:

Preheat your grill to medium-high heat.
Brush the halved romaine lettuce with olive oil and sprinkle with salt and black pepper.
Place the romaine halves on the preheated grill, cut side down.
Grill for about 2-3 minutes or until the edges are charred, and the lettuce is slightly wilted.

4. Assemble the Grilled Caesar Salad:

Place the grilled romaine halves on a serving platter.
Drizzle the Caesar dressing over the grilled lettuce.
Top with homemade croutons and grated Parmesan cheese.

5. Enjoy:

Serve the Grilled Caesar Salad immediately while the romaine is still warm. This twist on the classic Caesar salad adds a smoky flavor to the crisp lettuce, creating a delightful summer dish.

Smoked Mac and Cheese

Ingredients:

For the Smoked Mac and Cheese:

- 1 lb elbow macaroni or your favorite pasta
- 1/2 cup unsalted butter
- 1/2 cup all-purpose flour
- 4 cups milk
- 4 cups shredded sharp cheddar cheese
- 1 cup shredded mozzarella cheese
- 1/2 cup grated Parmesan cheese
- 1 teaspoon Dijon mustard
- 1 teaspoon garlic powder
- Salt and black pepper to taste
- 1 cup breadcrumbs (optional, for topping)

For Smoking:

- 2 cups wood chips (hickory, apple, or your preferred wood)
- Smoker or grill

Instructions:

1. Cook the Pasta:

    Cook the elbow macaroni according to the package instructions until al dente. Drain and set aside.

2. Prepare the Cheese Sauce:

    In a large saucepan, melt the butter over medium heat.
    Stir in the flour to create a roux. Cook for 1-2 minutes, stirring constantly.
    Gradually whisk in the milk to avoid lumps. Continue whisking until the mixture thickens.
    Reduce the heat to low, and stir in the shredded cheddar, mozzarella, and Parmesan cheeses until melted and smooth.
    Add Dijon mustard, garlic powder, salt, and black pepper. Adjust the seasonings to your liking.

3. Combine Pasta and Cheese Sauce:

   Add the cooked pasta to the cheese sauce, stirring to coat the pasta evenly. If you're using breadcrumbs, you can mix them into the mac and cheese for added texture or save them for the topping.

4. Smoking:

   Preheat your smoker or grill to 225°F (107°C).
   If using wood chips, soak them in water for about 30 minutes, then drain.
   Place the soaked wood chips in the smoker box or wrap them in aluminum foil, poking some holes to allow the smoke to escape.
   Transfer the mac and cheese to a heat-safe dish or disposable aluminum pan.
   Place the dish on the smoker or grill grates.
   Smoke the mac and cheese at 225°F (107°C) for about 1-2 hours or until it develops a smoky flavor. If you like a stronger smoke flavor, you can extend the smoking time.

5. Serve:

   Remove the smoked mac and cheese from the smoker or grill.
   Optionally, sprinkle breadcrumbs on top and broil in the oven for a few minutes until golden brown.
   Serve hot and enjoy the smoky, cheesy goodness!

Smoked Mac and Cheese is a crowd-pleaser that combines the creamy comfort of classic mac and cheese with a hint of smokiness.

Grilled Stuffed Jalapeños with Cream Cheese

Ingredients:

- 12 large jalapeño peppers, halved lengthwise and seeds removed
- 8 ounces cream cheese, softened
- 1 cup shredded cheddar cheese
- 1 teaspoon garlic powder
- 1 teaspoon onion powder
- 1/2 teaspoon smoked paprika
- 1/2 teaspoon cumin
- Salt and black pepper to taste
- 12 slices of bacon, cut in half
- Toothpicks

Instructions:

1. Prepare the Jalapeños:

    Preheat your grill to medium-high heat.
    Cut the jalapeños in half lengthwise, and use a spoon to scoop out the seeds and membranes. Be cautious with the jalapeños; you may want to wear gloves to protect your hands from the heat.

2. Prepare the Cream Cheese Filling:

    In a mixing bowl, combine the softened cream cheese, shredded cheddar cheese, garlic powder, onion powder, smoked paprika, cumin, salt, and black pepper. Mix until well combined.

3. Stuff the Jalapeños:

    Spoon the cream cheese mixture into each jalapeño half, pressing it down slightly.

4. Wrap with Bacon:

Wrap each cream cheese-stuffed jalapeño half with a half-slice of bacon, securing it with toothpicks.

5. Grill the Stuffed Jalapeños:

Place the stuffed jalapeños on the preheated grill.
Grill for about 15-20 minutes, turning occasionally, until the bacon is crispy and the jalapeños are tender.

6. Serve:

Remove the grilled stuffed jalapeños from the grill and let them cool for a few minutes.
Carefully remove the toothpicks.
Serve the stuffed jalapeños hot as a delightful and spicy appetizer.

7. Enjoy:

These Grilled Stuffed Jalapeños with Cream Cheese make for a perfect appetizer for parties or gatherings. The creamy filling balances the heat of the jalapeños, while the bacon adds a savory and crispy touch.

Barbecue Baked Beans with Bacon

Ingredients:

- 4 cans (15 ounces each) of navy beans or your preferred beans, drained and rinsed
- 8 slices bacon, cooked and crumbled
- 1 medium onion, finely chopped
- 1/2 cup barbecue sauce
- 1/4 cup ketchup
- 1/4 cup molasses
- 1/4 cup brown sugar, packed
- 2 tablespoons Dijon mustard
- 1 tablespoon apple cider vinegar
- 1 teaspoon Worcestershire sauce
- Salt and black pepper to taste

Instructions:

1. Preheat the Oven:

Preheat your oven to 350°F (175°C).

2. Cook the Bacon:

Cook the bacon until crispy, then crumble it into small pieces. Set aside.

3. Sauté the Onion:

In a skillet, sauté the finely chopped onion over medium heat until it becomes translucent. Set aside.

4. Prepare the Barbecue Baked Beans:

In a large mixing bowl, combine the drained and rinsed navy beans, crumbled bacon, sautéed onions, barbecue sauce, ketchup, molasses, brown sugar, Dijon mustard, apple cider vinegar, Worcestershire sauce, salt, and black pepper.
Mix all the ingredients until well combined.

5. Bake the Beans:

Transfer the bean mixture to a baking dish.
Bake in the preheated oven for about 45-60 minutes or until the beans are hot and bubbly, and the sauce has thickened.

6. Serve:

Remove from the oven and let it cool for a few minutes before serving.

7. Enjoy:

Serve these Barbecue Baked Beans with Bacon as a flavorful and comforting side dish at your next barbecue or family gathering. The combination of smoky bacon and sweet, tangy barbecue flavors will be a hit!

Grilled Avocado with Salsa

Ingredients:

For the Grilled Avocado:

- 2 ripe avocados
- Olive oil
- Salt and black pepper to taste
- Lime wedges (for serving)

For the Salsa:

- 1 cup diced tomatoes
- 1/4 cup diced red onion
- 1/4 cup chopped fresh cilantro
- 1 jalapeño, seeds removed and finely chopped
- 1 clove garlic, minced
- Juice of 1 lime
- Salt and black pepper to taste

Instructions:

1. Prepare the Salsa:

   In a bowl, combine diced tomatoes, diced red onion, chopped cilantro, chopped jalapeño, minced garlic, lime juice, salt, and black pepper. Mix well to make the salsa.
   Refrigerate the salsa while you prepare the grilled avocados to allow the flavors to meld.

2. Grill the Avocado:

   Preheat your grill to medium-high heat.
   Cut the avocados in half and remove the pits.
   Brush the avocado halves with olive oil and sprinkle with salt and black pepper.
   Place the avocado halves on the preheated grill, cut side down.
   Grill for about 2-3 minutes until you get grill marks and the avocados are slightly softened.

3. Assemble:

   Remove the grilled avocado halves from the grill and place them on a serving plate.
   Spoon the salsa into the center of each avocado half.

4. Serve:

Serve the Grilled Avocado with Salsa immediately, garnished with additional cilantro if desired. Provide lime wedges on the side for an extra burst of freshness.

5. Enjoy:

Enjoy this light and flavorful dish as an appetizer, side dish, or a healthy snack. The warmth from the grill enhances the creamy texture of the avocado, while the salsa adds a zesty kick.

Garlic Butter Grilled Naan Bread

Ingredients:

- 4 pieces of naan bread
- 1/2 cup unsalted butter, melted
- 3 cloves garlic, minced
- 2 tablespoons chopped fresh cilantro (optional)
- Salt to taste

Instructions:

1. Preheat the Grill:

Preheat your grill to medium-high heat.

2. Prepare the Garlic Butter:

In a small saucepan or microwave-safe bowl, melt the unsalted butter.
Add the minced garlic to the melted butter and stir well. You can sauté the garlic in a pan for a minute to infuse the butter with garlic flavor.

3. Brush Naan with Garlic Butter:

Brush one side of each naan bread with the garlic butter mixture using a pastry brush.
If desired, sprinkle chopped fresh cilantro over the buttered side.

4. Grill the Naan:

Place the naan, buttered side down, on the preheated grill.
Grill for about 2-3 minutes or until the bottom side is golden and has grill marks.
While the first side is grilling, brush the top side of the naan with more garlic butter.
Flip the naan and grill the other side until golden and has grill marks.

5. Serve:

Remove the garlic butter grilled naan bread from the grill and cut into wedges or serve whole.

6. Enjoy:

Serve the Garlic Butter Grilled Naan Bread warm, and enjoy the rich and flavorful combination of garlic, butter, and the smokiness from the grill. This makes a perfect accompaniment to various dishes or a delightful snack on its own.

Caprese Skewers with Balsamic Glaze

Ingredients:

- Cherry tomatoes
- Fresh mozzarella balls (bocconcini)
- Fresh basil leaves
- Balsamic glaze
- Extra-virgin olive oil
- Salt and black pepper to taste
- Wooden skewers

Instructions:

1. Prepare the Skewers:

    Soak wooden skewers in water for about 30 minutes to prevent them from burning on the grill.
    Assemble the skewers by threading a cherry tomato, a fresh mozzarella ball, and a fresh basil leaf onto each skewer. Repeat the process until you have as many skewers as you need.

2. Drizzle with Olive Oil:

    Arrange the assembled skewers on a serving platter.
    Drizzle extra-virgin olive oil over the skewers.

3. Season with Salt and Pepper:

Sprinkle the skewers with salt and black pepper to taste.

4. Drizzle with Balsamic Glaze:

Generously drizzle balsamic glaze over the caprese skewers. The balsamic glaze adds a sweet and tangy flavor to the dish.

5. Serve:

Serve the Caprese Skewers with Balsamic Glaze immediately, allowing your guests to enjoy the fresh and vibrant flavors.

6. Enjoy:

These caprese skewers make for a delightful appetizer or a refreshing addition to a summer gathering. The combination of tomatoes, fresh mozzarella, basil, and balsamic glaze creates a burst of flavors in every bite.

Grilled Watermelon Salad with Feta

Ingredients:

- 4 cups cubed seedless watermelon
- 1 cup crumbled feta cheese
- 1/4 cup fresh mint leaves, chopped
- 2 tablespoons extra-virgin olive oil
- 1 tablespoon balsamic glaze
- Salt and black pepper to taste

Instructions:

1. Preheat the Grill:

Preheat your grill to medium-high heat.

2. Grill the Watermelon:

Thread watermelon cubes onto skewers or place them directly on the grill grates.
Grill for about 2-3 minutes on each side or until grill marks form, but the watermelon remains juicy.
Remove the grilled watermelon from the skewers or grill and let them cool slightly.

3. Assemble the Salad:

In a large serving bowl, combine the grilled watermelon cubes, crumbled feta cheese, and chopped fresh mint leaves.
Drizzle extra-virgin olive oil over the salad.
Season with salt and black pepper to taste.

4. Drizzle with Balsamic Glaze:

Generously drizzle balsamic glaze over the grilled watermelon salad for a sweet and tangy finish.

5. Toss Gently:

Gently toss the salad ingredients together to combine and coat everything in the flavors.

6. Serve:

Serve the Grilled Watermelon Salad with Feta immediately, either as a side dish or a refreshing appetizer.

7. Enjoy:

Enjoy the unique combination of smoky grilled watermelon, creamy feta, and the brightness of mint. This salad is perfect for warm weather and will impress your guests with its unexpected flavors.

BBQ Grilled Potato Packets

Ingredients:

- 4 large potatoes, thinly sliced
- 1 large onion, thinly sliced
- 4 cloves garlic, minced
- 1/4 cup olive oil
- 1 teaspoon dried thyme
- 1 teaspoon dried rosemary
- Salt and black pepper to taste
- Aluminum foil

Instructions:

1. Preheat the Grill:

Preheat your grill to medium-high heat.

2. Prepare the Potato Packets:

   In a large bowl, combine the thinly sliced potatoes, thinly sliced onion, minced garlic, olive oil, dried thyme, dried rosemary, salt, and black pepper. Toss everything together until well coated.
   Tear off four large pieces of aluminum foil, each big enough to hold a portion of the potato mixture.
   Divide the potato mixture evenly among the foil pieces, placing it in the center of each piece.

3. Create the Packets:

   Fold the sides of the foil over the potato mixture and seal the edges to create packets.
   Ensure the packets are well-sealed to trap the steam inside.

4. Grill the Potato Packets:

   Place the foil packets on the preheated grill.

Grill for about 20-25 minutes, turning the packets occasionally to ensure even cooking.
Check for doneness by poking a potato with a fork. If it goes through easily, the potatoes are cooked.

5. Serve:

Carefully open the foil packets, and transfer the grilled potato mixture to a serving dish.

6. Enjoy:

Serve the BBQ Grilled Potato Packets hot as a flavorful and savory side dish to complement your grilled main course. The combination of grilled potatoes, onions, and herbs creates a tasty and satisfying addition to your barbecue.

Pimento Cheese-Stuffed Grilled Mushrooms

Ingredients:

- 1 pound large mushrooms, cleaned and stems removed
- 1 cup pimento cheese (store-bought or homemade)
- 2 tablespoons olive oil
- 1 teaspoon smoked paprika
- Salt and black pepper to taste
- Chopped fresh parsley for garnish (optional)

Instructions:

1. Preheat the Grill:

Preheat your grill to medium-high heat.

2. Prepare the Mushrooms:

   Clean the mushrooms and remove the stems, creating a hollow space for the filling.
   In a bowl, toss the mushroom caps with olive oil, smoked paprika, salt, and black pepper.

3. Stuff the Mushrooms:

   Fill each mushroom cap with a spoonful of pimento cheese, pressing it down gently.
   Ensure that the mushrooms are generously stuffed with the pimento cheese.

4. Grill the Stuffed Mushrooms:

   Place the stuffed mushrooms on the preheated grill.
   Grill for about 8-10 minutes or until the mushrooms are tender, and the pimento cheese is melted and slightly golden.

5. Garnish and Serve:

Remove the stuffed mushrooms from the grill and place them on a serving platter.
Garnish with chopped fresh parsley if desired.

6. Enjoy:

Serve the Pimento Cheese-Stuffed Grilled Mushrooms hot as a delicious and cheesy appetizer. These stuffed mushrooms are a crowd-pleaser and perfect for your next gathering or barbecue.

Sauces and Marinades:

Homemade BBQ Sauce with a Kick

Ingredients:

- 1 cup ketchup
- 1/4 cup apple cider vinegar
- 1/4 cup Worcestershire sauce
- 1/4 cup Dijon mustard
- 1/4 cup brown sugar, packed
- 2 tablespoons molasses
- 2 cloves garlic, minced
- 1 teaspoon onion powder
- 1 teaspoon smoked paprika
- 1/2 teaspoon cayenne pepper (adjust to taste for heat)
- Salt and black pepper to taste

Instructions:

1. Combine Ingredients:

    In a saucepan, combine ketchup, apple cider vinegar, Worcestershire sauce, Dijon mustard, brown sugar, molasses, minced garlic, onion powder, smoked paprika, cayenne pepper, salt, and black pepper.
    Whisk the ingredients together until well combined.

2. Simmer the Sauce:

    Place the saucepan over medium heat and bring the mixture to a simmer. Reduce the heat to low and let the sauce simmer for about 15-20 minutes, stirring occasionally, until it thickens and the flavors meld.

3. Adjust Seasoning:

    Taste the sauce and adjust the seasoning if needed. If you prefer more heat, you can add additional cayenne pepper.

4. Cool and Store:

Allow the BBQ sauce to cool before transferring it to a jar or container.
Store in the refrigerator for up to a few weeks.

5. Enjoy:

Use your homemade BBQ sauce with a kick as a marinade, basting sauce, or dipping sauce for grilled meats, burgers, chicken, or any dish that could use a flavorful and spicy kick.

Chimichurri Sauce for Grilled Meats

Ingredients:

- 1 cup fresh flat-leaf parsley, finely chopped
- 1/4 cup fresh cilantro, finely chopped
- 3 cloves garlic, minced
- 1/2 cup extra-virgin olive oil
- 1/4 cup red wine vinegar
- 1 tablespoon fresh oregano, finely chopped
- 1 teaspoon red pepper flakes (adjust to taste for heat)
- Salt and black pepper to taste

Instructions:

1. Prepare the Herbs:

    Finely chop the fresh flat-leaf parsley and cilantro.
    Chop the fresh oregano finely.

2. Mix the Ingredients:

    In a bowl, combine the chopped parsley, cilantro, minced garlic, and chopped oregano.
    Add red wine vinegar, extra-virgin olive oil, red pepper flakes, salt, and black pepper.
    Stir the ingredients together until well combined.

3. Let it Rest:

    Allow the chimichurri sauce to sit for at least 15-20 minutes before serving. This helps the flavors to meld and intensify.

4. Adjust Seasoning:

    Taste the chimichurri sauce and adjust the seasoning according to your preference. You can add more salt, pepper, or red pepper flakes for extra heat.

5. Serve:

Serve the chimichurri sauce as a condiment alongside grilled meats. It works well with beef, chicken, lamb, or even grilled vegetables.

6. Enjoy:

Drizzle the chimichurri sauce over your grilled meats or use it as a marinade for an extra burst of flavor. The freshness of the herbs and the acidity of the vinegar make it a delightful addition to grilled dishes.

Thai Peanut Sauce for Grilled Satay

Ingredients:

- 1/2 cup creamy peanut butter
- 3 tablespoons soy sauce
- 2 tablespoons rice vinegar
- 2 tablespoons lime juice
- 2 tablespoons brown sugar
- 1 tablespoon sesame oil
- 1 teaspoon fresh ginger, grated
- 1 clove garlic, minced
- 1/2 teaspoon red pepper flakes (adjust to taste)
- 1/4 cup coconut milk (optional, for a creamier sauce)
- Water (to adjust consistency)
- Chopped peanuts and cilantro for garnish (optional)

Instructions:

1. Combine Ingredients:

    In a bowl, whisk together peanut butter, soy sauce, rice vinegar, lime juice, brown sugar, sesame oil, grated ginger, minced garlic, and red pepper flakes.
    If you prefer a creamier sauce, add coconut milk and mix well.

2. Adjust Consistency:

    If the sauce is too thick, you can adjust the consistency by adding water, a tablespoon at a time, until you reach your desired thickness.

3. Adjust Seasoning:

    Taste the sauce and adjust the seasoning according to your preference. You can add more soy sauce, lime juice, or brown sugar if needed.

4. Garnish:

    If desired, garnish the peanut sauce with chopped peanuts and cilantro.

5. Serve:

Serve the Thai peanut sauce as a dipping sauce for grilled satay or as a delicious accompaniment to grilled chicken, beef, or tofu.

6. Enjoy:

Enjoy the rich and flavorful Thai peanut sauce with your grilled satay or other grilled dishes. The combination of peanut butter, soy sauce, and aromatic spices creates a savory and satisfying sauce.

Honey-Soy Glaze for Grilled Chicken

Ingredients:

- 1/4 cup soy sauce
- 2 tablespoons honey
- 2 tablespoons olive oil
- 1 tablespoon rice vinegar
- 2 cloves garlic, minced
- 1 teaspoon grated fresh ginger
- 1 teaspoon sesame oil (optional)
- Red pepper flakes or black pepper to taste (optional, for heat)
- Chopped green onions and sesame seeds for garnish (optional)

Instructions:

1. Combine Ingredients:

    In a bowl, whisk together soy sauce, honey, olive oil, rice vinegar, minced garlic, grated ginger, and sesame oil (if using).
    If you like a bit of heat, add red pepper flakes or black pepper to the glaze.

2. Mix Well:

    Mix the ingredients well until the honey is fully incorporated into the sauce.

3. Marinate or Glaze:

    Use the honey-soy glaze as a marinade for your chicken before grilling. Allow the chicken to marinate for at least 30 minutes to let the flavors infuse.
    Alternatively, you can use the glaze to baste the chicken while grilling. Reserve some of the glaze for brushing onto the chicken during the cooking process.

4. Grill the Chicken:

    Preheat your grill to medium-high heat.
    Grill the chicken until fully cooked, periodically brushing it with the honey-soy glaze for added flavor and a glossy finish.

5. Garnish:

Once the chicken is done, garnish with chopped green onions and sesame seeds if desired.

6. Serve:

Serve the grilled chicken with the honey-soy glaze, and enjoy the delightful combination of savory, sweet, and tangy flavors.

This honey-soy glaze is perfect for a variety of grilled proteins, including chicken thighs, breasts, or wings. It adds a delicious Asian-inspired flair to your grilled dishes.

Bourbon Maple Glaze for Grilled Pork

Ingredients:

- 1/4 cup bourbon
- 1/4 cup maple syrup
- 2 tablespoons soy sauce
- 2 tablespoons Dijon mustard
- 2 cloves garlic, minced
- 1 tablespoon olive oil
- Salt and black pepper to taste
- Optional: 1 teaspoon Worcestershire sauce for an extra savory kick

Instructions:

1. Combine Ingredients:

    In a bowl, whisk together bourbon, maple syrup, soy sauce, Dijon mustard, minced garlic, olive oil, and Worcestershire sauce (if using).

2. Mix Well:

    Mix the ingredients well to ensure the bourbon, maple syrup, and other components are fully combined.

3. Season:

    Taste the glaze and adjust the seasoning if needed. Add salt and black pepper to taste.

4. Marinate or Glaze:

    Use the bourbon maple glaze as a marinade for your pork before grilling. Allow the pork to marinate for at least 30 minutes for the flavors to meld. Alternatively, use the glaze to baste the pork while grilling. Reserve some of the glaze for brushing onto the pork during the cooking process.

5. Grill the Pork:

Preheat your grill to medium-high heat.
Grill the pork until fully cooked, periodically brushing it with the bourbon maple glaze for a delicious caramelized finish.

6. Rest and Serve:

Allow the grilled pork to rest for a few minutes before slicing.
Serve the bourbon maple-glazed pork with any remaining glaze drizzled on top.

7. Enjoy:

Enjoy the succulent and flavorful grilled pork with the rich notes of bourbon and the sweetness of maple. This glaze works particularly well with pork chops, tenderloin, or ribs.